COLORADO
Wet & Wild

A Photographic Portfolio
by Todd Caudle

Skyline Press
Colorado Springs, Colorado

COLORADO
Wet & Wild

A Photographic Portfolio
by Todd Caudle

FRONT COVER, BACKGROUND: Waterfall detail, Sneffels Creek, San Juan Mountains
FRONT COVER, INSET: Sunrise reflection, Crestone Needle, Sangre de Cristo Wilderness
PREVIOUS PAGE: Sneffels Creek below Potosi Peak, Sneffels Range, San Juan Mountains
FACING PAGE: Dawn colors over Trappers Lake, Flat Tops Wilderness

Skyline Press
P. O. Box 26055
Colorado Springs, CO 80936

Foreword

In the spring of 1994 I set out for the high country with a mission -- to photograph as many of Colorado's lakes, creeks, waterfalls and reflections as I could before frigid temperatures returned to lock those subjects away for another winter. When I first conceived the idea for "Colorado Wet & Wild," my plan was to compile this portfolio over the course of two years. Even still, I suspected I'd have to supplement the hard work of two years with many photos from previous years, just to be able to publish a substantial collection of diverse images and locations.

To the contrary, the summer of '94 yielded so much magical light, and the Colorado wilds offered so many extraordinary photographic opportunities, that this book became a reality a year sooner than I'd planned. Indeed, over seventy-five percent of the photographs in this book were taken between June and October of that year.

In compiling this portfolio, it was necessary to explore many of the state's high cirque basins, where ancient glaciation and recession has carved a variety of bowls in the landscape and filled them with the clearest water you'll ever see. As I traveled across Colorado to photograph the scenes in this book, the diversity of these headwaters struck me. Some were lined with the richest, greenest grass I'd ever seen, while others were set in alpine basins so barren that, if not for the water and the crystal blue skies reflected in it, they'd have looked more like moonscapes. Some were tucked against fantastic, 1,000-foot headwalls, sheltering snow drifts that wouldn't see the sun all day. Still others were in vast beaver meadows that left the entire area with the consistency of a wet sponge. In each I found a unique beauty.

Water is a precious commodity in Colorado. It's hard to imagine what life here would be like without the mountains retaining most of their wet bounty of winter snow, to be withdrawn incrementally as temperatures rise.

It's amazing to me just how nature has the ability to replenish itself. Where did the moisture for all that snow originate? Blizzards in the Himalaya? Tropical storms on the equator? And where will the water in the lakes and creeks depicted in this book go once the sun has evaporated it and sent it on its way? Thunderheads over Kansas? Fog over London? One never knows.

Such is the endless cycle of nature.

— Todd Caudle
Colorado Springs

FACING PAGE: Reflection of an unnamed peak, along the Piney River, Eagles Nest Wilderness

Clearing storm over The Loch,
Rocky Mountain National Park

Spruce Creek descends from Mohawk Lakes, Tenmile Range
FACING PAGE: Frozen tarn, Independence Pass, Sawatch Range

Lily pads on Nymph Lake, Rocky Mountain National Park
FACING PAGE: Cascade on Mosquito Creek, below Mount Buckskin, Mosquito Range

Heartleaf arnica along the Roaring Fork River, Hunter-Fryingpan Wilderness
FACING PAGE: Cathedral Peak reflects in an alpine tarn, Maroon Bells-Snowmass Wilderness

Continental Falls below Mount Helen, Tenmile Range
FACING PAGE: Headwaters of Castle Creek, below Castle Peak, Elk Mountains

Along the shore of Lake Katherine, Mount Zirkel Wilderness
FACING PAGE: Alpine tarn below South Lookout Peak, Paradise Basin, San Juan Mountains

Willow Creek tumbles into lower Willow Creek Lake, Sangre de Cristo Wilderness
FACING PAGE: Late-day light and clearing storm on Marble Mountain, Sangre de Cristo Wilderness

Aspen trees along Castle Creek, White River National Forest
FACING PAGE: Evening sky reflection in Sheep Lake, Horseshoe Park, Rocky Mountain National Park
OVERLEAF: Pikes Peak reflects in a temporary pool atop Rampart Range

Snowmass Mountain and Geneva Lake, Maroon Bells-Snowmass Wilderness
FACING PAGE: Breaking Storm over Peak Two, Weminuche Wilderness

Sunset light on Mount Bross, Mosquito Range
FACING PAGE: Sunrise clouds over lower Mohawk Lake, Tenmile Range

A transitory pool surrounded by marsh marigolds, Mosquito Range
FACING PAGE: Headwaters of Stevens Creek, along the Grays Peak Trail

Early-season snow on Green Mountain, Stony Pass, San Juan Mountains
FACING PAGE: Cascade below Emerald Lake, Tyndall Gorge, Rocky Mountain National Park

Autumn colors frame Whitmore Falls, below Engineer Pass, San Juan Mountains
FACING PAGE: A golden aspen forest mirrored in a beaver pond below Mount Elbert, Sawatch Range

Scree-filled Kite Lake reflects partly cloudy skies, San Juan Mountains
FACING PAGE: Edith Mountain below Cinnamon Pass, American Basin, San Juan Mountains

A series of shelf lakes along the Colorado Trail, Weminuche Wilderness
FACING PAGE: Mount Democrat's southern ramparts at sunrise, Lake Emma, Mosquito Range
OVERLEAF: Snow-ringed beaver ponds along the headwaters of the North Fork South Arkansas River, Sawatch Range

The tranquility of evening light below White Dome, Weminuche Wilderness
FACING PAGE: Morning clouds obscure the summit of Crestone Needle, Sangre de Cristo Wilderness

A shelf lake high above Lake Agnes reflects afternoon light, Colorado State Forest
FACING PAGE: A rocky tarn below Mount Edwards, Stevens Gulch, along the Grays Peak Trail

44

Peak Three and Peak Two rise high above numerous lakes in the Weminuche Wilderness
FACING PAGE: A taste of winter, Denver Lake below Engineer Pass, San Juan Mountains

A double image of fall colors at Cushman Lake, San Juan Mountains
FACING PAGE: Golden aspens frame Nellie Creek Falls, Uncompahgre National Forest

Spring runoff tunnels through winter snow, below Linkins Lake, Hunter-Fryingpan Wilderness
FACING PAGE: Cascade below Twining Peak, Hunter-Fryingpan Wilderness

Lily Lake in winter, Rocky Mountain National Park
FACING PAGE: Snow pillows in Sneffels Creek, San Juan Mountains

Symmetrical shadow on the shore of Cathedral Lake, Maroon Bells-Snowmass Wilderness
FACING PAGE: Lush fall colors along the headwaters of the Rio Grande, San Juan Mountains
OVERLEAF: Independence Lake mirrors approaching storm clouds, Hunter-Fryingpan Wilderness

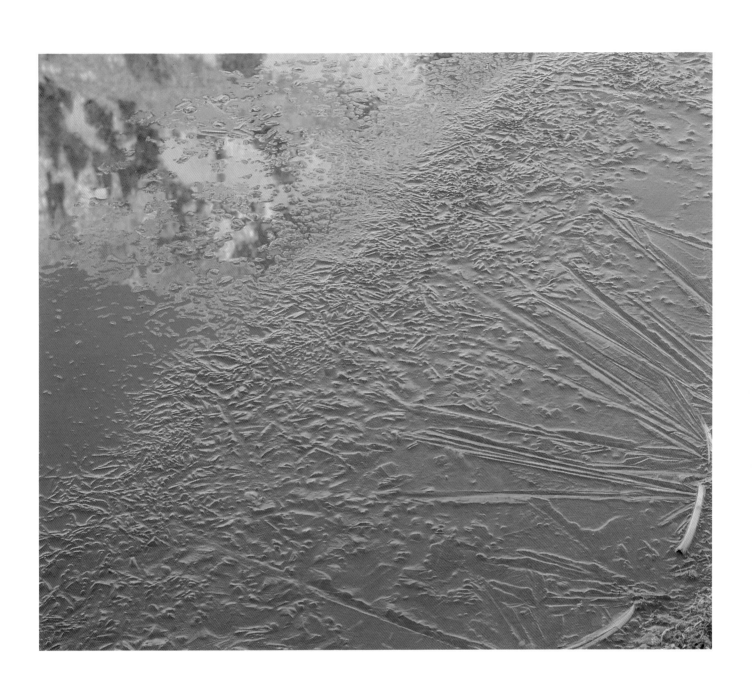

Icy surface of a small tarn, White River National Forest
FACING PAGE: Frozen waters of Medano Creek below Mount Herard, Great Sand Dunes National Monument

Subalpine grasses and Gore Range reflection, Eagles Nest Wilderness
FACING PAGE: Mount Democrat and the outflow of Kite Lake, Mosquito Range

A double waterfall along the Roaring Fork River, Hunter-Fryingpan Wilderness
FACING PAGE: Snowmelt-fed waters of South Mineral Creek, San Juan Mountains

Two views; Maroon Bells and Maroon Lake, Elk Mountains

Storm clouds thicken high above South Mineral Creek, San Juan Mountains
FACING PAGE: Day's end below Engineer Pass, San Juan Mountains

Waterfall along Castle Creek, White River National Forest
FACING PAGE: The Crags in American Basin, San Juan Mountains

Waterfall below Lake Emma, Mosquito Range
FACING PAGE: North Clear Creek Falls in fog, Rio Grande National Forest

Reflections of the Gore Range along the Piney River,
Eagles Nest Wilderness

Grass-ringed beaver pond below Independence Pass, Sawatch Range
FACING PAGE: Symmetrical reflection of an unnamed peak, Paradise Basin, San Juan Mountains

74

Sunrise at Spruce Lake, along the Continental Divide Trail, Weminuche Wilderness
FACING PAGE: Archuleta Lake, along the Continental Divide Trail, Weminuche Wilderness
OVERLEAF: Last light on Ute Ridge, Kite Lake, San Juan Mountains